CPA FIRM MANAGEMENT & GOVERNANCE

Marc Rosenberg, CPA

MONOGRAPHS BY MARC ROSENBERG

CPA Firm Succession Planning: A Perfect Storm

How to Bring In New Partners

How to Negotiate a CPA Firm Merger

How to Operate a Compensation Committee

What Really Makes CPA Firms Profitable?

Guide to Planning the Firm Retreat

Effective Partner Relations and Communications

Strategic Planning and Goal Setting For Results

For more information or to purchase additional titles visit:
www.rosenbergassoc.com + click on
"Monographs by Marc Rosenberg"

Connect with Marc:
marc@rosenbergassoc.com
blog.rosenbergassoc.com

CPA FIRM MANAGEMENT & GOVERNANCE

Marc Rosenberg, CPA

Copyright 2012
The Rosenberg Associates Ltd.
1000 Skokie Boulevard, Suite 555
Wilmette, IL 60091

TABLE OF CONTENTS

1

Introduction

If I were writing this monograph prior to, say, 2005, the title would simply be "How to Manage a CPA Firm." But in recent years, a new term has come into vogue: Firm Governance.

As I pondered ideas for this introduction, I gave a lot of thought to what "governance" means, what "management" means, how they are alike and how they are different.

I sought out the opinions of several well-known national CPA firm consultants and their responses were, as always, enlightening and insightful. Their major sentiments were:

1. Today, when people use the term "firm governance," they're referring to formal, written rules and bylaws for making decisions such as voting and defining authorities of the MP and other individuals and committees. Two of my colleagues summed it up with "who does what."

2. "Management" is the execution of decisions, which includes implementation of goals, policies, procedures, planning, managing people, improving their performance and holding people accountable. Management is the process of making sure everyone knows what to do and managing them to make sure it gets done. My thanks to **Charles Hylan, CPA** of St. Louis-based The Growth Partnership, for the bulk of this paragraph.

Until the time that "governance" became a buzz word, there was very little thought given to the distinction between these two terms. Management was clearly the all-encompassing term, with governance being a subset of it.

So there you have it. Using the above definitions, this monograph addresses both areas quite heavily.

I would like to share two particularly insightful quotes from my colleagues:

> "Leadership is a whole other subject. I once read that if you want to understand the difference between leaders and managers you look to where their power comes from. Leaders derive their power from the consent of the people (partners). Managers derive their power from the organizational hierarchy. Leaders do not need titles. Managers always have titles." Denver-based CPA firm consultant **Rich Rinehart of Grant Partners.**

> "What we consultants think is not as important as what the client has in mind when he/she uses the firm governance phrase. I believe you will learn a lot about what is going on with that client if you ask "What does that phrase mean to you?" Sedona, AZ-based CPA firm consultant **Dr. Bob Martin.**

My thanks to several other nationally renowned CPA firm consultants who contributed to this introduction: Chicago-based Allan Koltin of Koltin Consulting, Rita Keller of Keller Advisors in Dayton, Connecticut-based Steve Weinstein, Steve Erickson of Albuquerque, Phoenix-based Roman Kepczyk of Xcentric and Gordon Gilchrist from the 2020 Group in the U.K.

2

Management & Leadership

While the differentiation of management from governance is really an issue of professional jargon, a discussion of "management vs. "leadership" is a more substantive matter. During my 30+ year career in the business world, I have read many books and articles and heard many speeches on these two subjects that are near and dear to my heart. Here is a very short list of my favorite definitions of management and leadership.

Management's job is to:
- Decide what you want to be (plan) and make it happen (implement).
- Hold others accountable for their performance.
- Create an environment in which firm personnel can be successful and achieve their goals.

"While leadership decides what "first things" are, it is management that puts them first - day by day, moment by moment. Management is discipline; carrying it out."   Stephen Covey.

Management is getting results through other people.

Important management functions:

- Hit the firm's top and bottom line targets.
- Carry out the firm's business plan.

- Ensure that people meet personal goals that are linked to the firm's overall goals.
- Establish systems of accountability.
- Solve problems swiftly as they arise.
- Be a cheerleader to the troops.
- Remove obstacles for co-workers.

Leadership identifies challenges & focuses people's attention on those challenges.   Ronald Heifetz.

Leadership is coping with change. Management is coping with complexity.

Leadership controls people by pushing them in the right direction; leadership motivates them by satisfying basic human needs.

Leadership is visionary. Leaders are constantly finding new things that the firm needs to be doing, stretching the abilities and imaginations of everyone.

Real leaders possess real convictions - strong feelings that build up over time. If those convictions match the requirements of a group of followers, then great leadership emerges.

Leadership is crucial for facilitating change in organizations because people need help in overcoming their natural resistance to change.

Leadership is the ability to establish a powerful relationship with a subordinate or a peer that will motivate and inspire that person to commit wholeheartedly and passionately and with dedication to the challenges the leader needs to solve which will, in turn, solve the problem of the follower.

Management is a people job. If you're not up to the task of working with people – helping them, listening to them, encouraging them and guiding them – then you shouldn't be a manager.   Bob Nelson and Peter Economy.

******

When reading the above quotes on management and leadership, it seems we are being told that the two traits are almost mutually exclusive, like black and white. Yes, it's true that many inspiring, innovative leaders are lousy managers because they don't have the focus and discipline required to manage. And some managers make terrible leaders because either they lack the necessary interpersonal skills or over-rely on titles, authority and intimidation to get people to follow.

But in every walk of life, there are a lot of managers who are *also* good leaders and vice versa. I have had the good fortune to work with many of them. It *can* be done.

Many CPA firm partners confuse *charisma* with *leadership*. Jim Collins in his book *Good To Great,* clarified this nicely:

> "Good-to-great leaders...are often self-effacing, quiet, reserved, even shy, a paradoxical blend of personal humility and professional will. They act with quiet, calm determination, relying principally on inspired standards, not inspiring charisma, to motivate.

> Darwin Smith, former CEO of Kimberly-Clark said: "I never stopped trying to become qualified for the job."

Leadership vs. Management vs. Administration

When attending conferences, we love "aha" moments. Those are moments when a speaker says something so profound that it causes a sudden understanding of a major issue and captures our imagination. We can't wait to get back to the office, share it with our partners and start implementing the idea.

I had an "aha" moment in 2005 or so. The speaker was Bob Bunting, long time MP of west coast regional firm Moss Adams, a leader in our profession par excellence. He delivered a very simple but powerful statement that described a value system at Moss Adams:

- Leadership is worth MORE than your billing rate.
- Management is worth your billing rate.
- Administration is worth LESS than your billing rate.

My take on this is:

1. The most important thing a partner can do is lead. It's worth more than management, bringing in business or managing clients.
2. Hours spent managing the firm, an office or department are just as valuable as a billable hours.
3. Administration is important, but not as important as management because the former can be performed by a non-partner at a fraction of what a typical partner earns. Partners should not be doing administration. More on this later in this monograph.

I've taken the liberty of converting Bunting's "aha" moment into the chart on the next page.

Leadership vs. Management vs. Administration

Leadership	Worth **MORE** than your billing rate.	<ul><li>Identifies challenges.</li><li>Gets people to follow.</li><li>Builds strong culture.</li><li>Visionary.</li><li>Inspires and energizes people.</li><li>Copes with change.</li></ul>
Management	Worth your billing rate.	<ul><li>Plan and implement.</li><li>Hold people accountable.</li><li>Solves problems quickly.</li><li>P&L management.</li><li>Copes with complexity.</li></ul>
Administration	Worth **LESS** than your billing rate.	<ul><li>Focus is on day to day.</li><li>Monitor/report on results.</li><li>Operate systems.</li><li>Policies and procedures.</li><li>Support role.</li></ul>

Management vs. Administration

These two terms have been erroneously used interchangeably over the years, but they are quite different. Here is a concise summary of the distinctions.

Management's job is to ...	Administration's job is to ...
• Decide what you want to be (plan) and make it happen (implement).	• Focus on the day-to-day, putting first things first.
• Lead. Foster collegiality, a strong culture and team spirit; get people to follow.	• Monitor and report operating results (keep score).
• Help firm personnel realize their potential.	• Operate, maintain and upgrade systems.
• Impact the performance and behavior of the partners; partner accountability.	• Create, enforce and interpret policy.
• Create an environment in which people can be successful.	• Support practice personnel by providing them with an efficient, comfortable work environment, thereby enhancing their productivity.
• Leverage their time so that every hour they work creates multiple hours of work and opportunities for others.	

Partners should stay out of administration and leave it to firm administrators, COOs or office managers.

MANAGEMENT PHILOSOPHY
OF CPA FIRMS

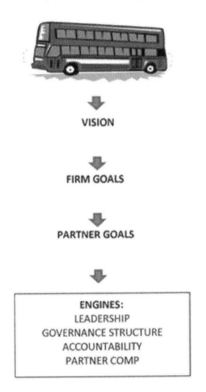

VISION

FIRM GOALS

PARTNER GOALS

ENGINES:
LEADERSHIP
GOVERNANCE STRUCTURE
ACCOUNTABILITY
PARTNER COMP

Management philosophy of a CPA firm

I have used the above flowchart for nearly 20 years and it has not lost one iota of relevance in demonstrating how to <u>effectively</u> manage a CPA firm. Its message is simple yet powerful.

Most firms make the mistake of managing from the <u>bottom</u> of the chart, and try to work their way up. The firm is primarily managed by:

- Appointing a managing partner who usually is the guy with the biggest book of business but often is a lousy manager.

- Allocating income based on an "eat what you kill" mentality. The partners reason that altering the size of one's paycheck is the best way to provide feedback to a partner which will, in turn, lead to improved performance.

There are many flaws to this management approach, a couple of which are:

1. How can you compensate partners if you don't identify what you want to pay them *for*?

2. How can a firm ever expect to attain its vision and strategic goals if achievement of those goals isn't strongly linked with partners' compensation?

The correct way to manage a firm is, of course, to start at the <u>top</u>. Let's skip the bus at the top of the chart for now and start with **VISION.** The firm looks at where they are now and where they want to be in 5 years, concluding with the creation of a vision statement that clearly describes what they would like the firm to look like in 5 years, in very specific terms. This is where management begins.

Next, the firm decides what **FIRM GOALS** and actions are needed to achieve the vision.

At this stage the firm acknowledges that "the firm" can't do *anything*. The **PARTNERS** and other key personnel need to be assigned roles in achieving the firm **GOALS**.

Up to this point, the firm is like an automobile whose engine hasn't been turned on. The 4 items in the **ENGINES** box represent the ignition that energizes and propels the firm to implementing the vision:

- **Leadership**. Every plan must have a champion.

- **Management structure.** The partners have a critically important role in the firm: to provide fantastic service to a large volume of clients and to bring in new business. The partners won't have any time to implement strategic plan goals unless the firm has a management structure in place which provides the support needed by the partners to function effectively.

- **Accountability.** This is probably the biggest reason why CPA firms fail to implement the vision. Firms must have systems in place to hold partners accountable for the parts they play in helping the firm achieve its vision.

- **Partner compensation.** The firm needs to allocate income based on the relative success each partner has in achieving goals and helping the firm achieve its vision.

Now, back to the bus at the top of the chart. The bus relates to one of the most often-cited business quotes of the last 50 years. This passage comes from Jim Collins' legendary *Good To Great*:

> "Great organizations did not *first* figure out where to drive the bus and then get people to take it there. Instead, they *first* got the right people off the bus and *then* figured out where to drive it. People either stay on the bus for a long time or they get off in a hurry."

Some firms have partners who are always saying negative things like:

- "That will never work."
- "We've tried that before and it failed."
- "Goal setting is a waste of time."

These people zap everyone's energy and make people doubt the value of management and strategic planning, thereby making it difficult to rally the troops on the firm's game plan. They must leave the firm or be confined to the periphery before strategic planning can start.

Many firms aren't willing to confront these naysayers and hold them in check. But these negative people will sabotage the firm's efforts to manage effectively.

3

Styles of Management

In the context of this chapter, the terms "partnership" and "corporate" are used to describe a management style rather than legal entities such as partnership, corporation, LLC, etc.

Partnership vs. corporate style

In our work with CPA firms, we have observed two distinct styles of management: partnership and corporate.

Partnership style. Democracy heavily impacts the way partnerships are governed. In a democracy, every partner has a vote and there is a "majority rules" mentality. Checks and balances prevent leaders from becoming dictators. The "citizens" want a reasonable amount of input into decisions.

In a partnership style, partners have "certain inalienable rights" like:
- The right to vote on all major and many minor decisions.
- The right to be "involved" in most things that are "going on."
- The right *not* to be accountable. (No one admits this, of course).

The partnership style is often synonymous with "management by committee." As is the case with most committees, decisions are frequently watered down because they are the result of compromises necessary to get everyone to agree. And the effort required to achieve the compromise always slows down the decision-making process.

A by-product of the partnership style is a feeling by the partners, sometimes subconscious, that "rank hath its privilege:"

1. Many feel that becoming a partner means one has "made it," and has earned the privilege of making his/her own decisions and to never have those decisions questioned; kind of like royalty.

2. A belief that "this is a profession," where the most valued attributes are technical excellence, expertise and professionalism. Partners have collegial relationships, unlike in a bureaucracy. Partners have earned their status and inherently know what to do and how to do it. No one needs to "manage" them because the fact that they have attained partner status means they can and should manage themselves.

Some partners openly acknowledge and espouse these rights while others exercise them more discreetly.

Corporate style. In many ways, the corporate style is the polar opposite of partnership style. With corporate style governance, duties, decisions and authority are vested in a few people. In a CPA firm, the corporate style is driven by a critical belief:

Partners are very busy people with two primary duties: managing clients (including developing new clients) and helping staff grow. These duties are critically important to a firm's success.

If we couple this belief with the fact that many partners don't have the skills to manage the firm, it makes good sense to appoint someone (a managing partner) or a small group of people (an executive committee or Board) with the management and leadership skills and the time necessary to manage the firm.

Unfortunately, the word "corporate" has an inherently unpleasant sound to it. To partners, it may feel like loss of control and taking away their rights as partners to be involved in everything and to be informed of what's going on. Some partners fear that a corporate style makes them feel like an employee instead of an owner.

14

Over the years, we have conducted a word recognition exercise with many partner groups contemplating changes in their governance structure. We ask them to think of words that pop into their minds when the terms "partnership" and "corporation" are uttered.

The results of this exercise are shown below.

Words Commonly Used To Describe "Partnership Style" vs. "Corporate Style" Governance

Partnership style

BENEFITS	POSSIBLE NEGATIVES
Collegiality	Management by committee
Feel like an owner	Watered down decisions
Teamwork	Difficult to get consensus
Joint decision making	Hard to get everyone together
Having input; participative	No one in charge
Sharing	Decisions don't get made or are
Resources	made slowly
Help	Promotes feeling of entitlement
Freedom to exercise my own	Over-reliance on one's rank
judgment	No accountability
"I've made it;" rank	Inconsistencies in work, policies
Democratic	Reactive

Corporate style

BENEFITS	POSSIBLE NEGATIVES
Efficient	Not involved in decision-making
Profit-making	People telling us what to do
Leadership	Feeling left out
Clarity	Autocratic
Consistent and efficient	Policies and procedures
Setting priorities	Reduces collegiality
Accountability	Heavy handed; ruthless
Decision-making	Accountability
Structure; organization chart	Empire building
Managing partner	Don't approve of decisions or
Success	style
Proactive	Big brother; lots of rules
	Political

Firm size plays an important role in deciding which of the two styles to adopt. A 2-5 partner firm is small enough to be managed successfully in the partnership style. (For now, let's assume "successful" means growing vs. stagnating, attaining solid profit levels and having an above average staff.) At this size, the partner group is small enough to function well as a democracy, not requiring the same level of sophistication as a larger firm.

Here are a few examples (there are many others):

1. Scheduling. The partners simply stroll to the staff bullpen and grab a body that's in the office that day.

2. Marketing. Near-total reliance on the partners' individual willingness and ability to do practice development. This *can* work at a small firm.

3. Management and administration. Each partner pitches in, thereby precluding the need for a managing partner and a firm

16

administrator (the firm may have a "managing partner," but it's mostly a cosmetic position). Also, because there are just a handful of partners, it's more likely that they see eye to eye with each other and find it easier to arrive at decisions, thus avoiding the "herding cats" phenomenon that plagues larger partner groups.

4. Decisions. When something important comes up, there are few enough partners to quickly huddle together on a moment's notice and make a decision.

5. Leadership development. The owners would *prefer* the exit strategy of developing staff into partners who buy them out vs. merging. But in the back of their minds, they reason that they can spend 30 years as a partner, make good money, enjoy their work, all while operating as big fish in a little pond. Should they fail to develop future leaders, they figure they can always merge into a larger firm. This exit strategy has become less viable as buyers are increasingly able to cherry-pick merger candidates from the plethora of firms looking to sell, but this is a subject for another time.

Once the size of the partner group moves beyond 5 partners and gets to 7 or 8 owners, all of the above become increasingly more difficult. Eventually, chaos reigns supreme until the firm realizes that it needs more formality and structure in its management.

There are many reasons why the Top 100 firms are the Top 100 (the 100th largest firm in 2012 was roughly $30M and virtually all had at least 15 partners). One is their commitment to management. It is literally impossible to effectively manage a firm of this size in "partnership" mode and enjoy growth and profitability. The organization is simply too big.

Being a partner at a firm managed with a corporate style has little or nothing to do with title or "involvement" in management. Instead, being a partner is characterized by:

1. Bringing in business.
2. Mentoring and developing staff into partners.
3. Managing, retaining and growing a significant client base.
4. Leveraging work by pushing it down to others.
5. Being the firm's go-to person for a critical function such as a service, industry or technical skill.
6. Assisting the firm achieve its overall vision.
7. Driving the firm's profits and overall success as a result of the above.

At corporate style firms, partners enjoy not being involved in management, thankful that others do it. Partners enjoy not attending boring, frustrating, unproductive partner meetings, content that one to three full partner meetings a year is sufficient to keep them informed of what's going on in the firm. One of the reasons they enjoy these things is the time it frees up to focus on the seven functions above.

Choosing between a partnership and corporate style doesn't mean that there is a right answer and a wrong answer. It is simply a choice that partner groups make.

Tight ship vs. "loosey-goosey"

This may simply be a variation of the partnership vs. corporate style discussion, but I want to address it nonetheless.

Tight ship. An approach to firm management that embraces written policies and procedures, both technically and administratively. Policies are consistent from partner to partner so that all personnel get the same message and pull in the same direction. Everyone's role is clear. Measurable goals are created and achieved because accomplishing them is assigned to specific individuals with accountability.

Some of you reading this may be fearful that running a tight-ship sounds intrusive, bureaucratic, overbearing, stifles innovation and greatly limits one's judgment and freedom to perform. This is not the case.

- Tight-ship firms simply want to have efficient processes and operate smoothly, while still giving its people the latitude to exercise judgment and common sense in how they work.

- When tight-ship firms develop a goal, they understand that the accomplishment of the goal will be greatly enhanced if they focus on it, devote the resources to accomplish it and establish accountability for it, *instead of* "wishing" for the goal to happen.

"Loosey-goosey." An approach to firm management adopted due to the partners' dislike of bureaucracy, formality, goals, to-do lists, etc. Each partner feels that being a partner gives them the right to decide what they do, when they do it and how often they change their mind. They don't like goals and procedures because they want to reserve the right *not* to follow them if they choose to do so, and they don't want to be held accountable for this.

The tone of the above may sound biased on my part. If a firm's partners are happy being loosey-goosey, enjoy their work, are satisfied with their income and can tolerate the inefficiencies of being "loosey-goosey," then who am I to question their decision?

4

The Managing Partner

After deciding on a management style for the firm, the next issue for the partners to decide is how the firm will be managed.

The first question is: Do we want the firm managed by a leader, which for a CPA firm is the Managing Partner (MP) or managed by one or more committees of partners?

The case for having a leader

D. Quinn Mills, in his *Leadership: How to Lead, How to Live (2005)*, states the case nicely for why organizations need leaders:

> Few things are more important to human activity than leadership. Effective leadership helps our nation through times of peril. It makes a business successful. It enables a not-for-profit organization to fulfill its mission. The effective leadership of parents enables children to grow strong and healthy and become productive adults.
>
> The absence of leadership is equally dramatic. Without leadership, organizations move too slowly, stagnate, and lose their way. Much of the literature about organizations stresses decision-making and implies that if decision-making is timely, complete, and correct, then things will go well. Yet a decision by itself changes nothing.

After a decision is made, an organization faces the problem of implementation—how to get things done in a timely and effective way.

Problems of implementation are really issues about how leaders influence behavior, change the course of events, and overcome resistance. Leadership is crucial in implementing decisions successfully.

Management by committee

Most organizations find that management by committee is not a good way to efficiently run a business. CPA firms are no exception. Here is a chart listing various reasons partners give for preferring management by committee over a MP, and a rebuttal for each reason:

Reasons to Manage By Committee Instead of Having an MP	Rebuttal
1. We don't want one person with too much power. We like decisions made by "majority rules." Having a MP would remove democracy from the decision-making process and deny us our vote.	Running a business is not a democracy. Partners should be taking great care of clients & staff. Leave management to the MP. If the MP job is structured properly, there won't be abuse of power.
2. We don't have anyone who has the ability or charisma to be the MP. Several heads are better than one.	Jim Collins says great leaders are self-effacing. They act with quiet, calm and determination, relying on inspired standards, not charisma, to motivate.
3. No one wants to be the MP. We all love our client work and being the MP will take us away from that.	If no one wants to be MP, hire an outside CEO or COO to run the firm, reporting to a Board.
4. No one has the time to be MP. Let's spread the administrative burden over several of us.	Having partners carve up the firm administrator's job actually *reduces* profits because the cost of reducing partners' client time *exceeds* the administrator's cost.
5. Our rainmaker would be our best MP. But we'll lose money if our rainmaker does less selling and more managing.	The best MPs do 3 things: bring in business, manage partner performance and play a leadership role with the firm's larger clients, with relatively low billable hours.

What a Managing Partner is...and is *not*
Or...
Why firms need a Managing Partner

Over the years, I have found that many firms lack a clear understanding of what a Managing Partner is. Often, it's a negative conception, caused by a bad experience at their current firm or a previous one. So, to avoid a repeat of these bad experiences, the partners decide either not to have a MP or to provide for the MP position with greatly limited authority and responsibility.

The points below clarify what a Managing Partner IS and IS NOT

A Managing Partner IS NOT:

1. A dictator.
2. The sole decision maker on all key issues.
3. The only person to confront or resolve the firm's problems.
4. Necessarily the only or even the best marketer.
5. Effective if partners expect to be consulted on all minor issues.
6. The only one who has agenda items for partner meetings.
7. The firm administrator.
8. A full time job (though it could be if this is best for the firm).

A Managing Partner IS:

1. A visionary.
2. A leader (though rarely charismatic).
3. Focuses people on "first things."
4. Gets decisions made promptly.
5. Focuses on achieving revenue, productivity and profitability goals.
6. Holds partners accountable.
7. Makes sure that the firm markets.
8. Makes the firm a fantastic place for staff to work.

Two types of managing partners

"True" managing partner. See the MP job description on the next page. The "true" MP manages every aspect of the firm, especially managing partner performance and behavior and managing the firm's growth and profitability. A true CEO.

Administrative partner. A MP that performs the job description on the next page except managing partner performance and the firm's growth and profitability.

There are two main scenarios that explain why firms have an administrative-type MP instead of a true MP:

1. The partners don't *expect* the MP to manage partner performance and hold them accountable.
2. The partners don't *want* the MP to manage partner performance and hold them accountable.
3. The MP doesn't have the skills or desire to manage other partners and hold them accountable.

If a MP does not manage partner performance, it's very difficult to have a meaningful impact on growth and profitability because it's primarily the performance of partners that drives a firm's performance.

Even though the administrative partner doesn't impact partner performance, this person still provides value in other ways:

1. Keeps the peace. The MP may not be able to *manage* partners, but his/her credibility keeps the partner group together and resolves disputes among partners.

2. Every firm needs a public face in the community and with the staff.

3. The MP still performs critical tasks such as strategic planning, supervising a management team and running partner meetings.

MANAGING PARTNER
JOB DESCRIPTION

1. The firm's chief executive officer. Provides leadership.

2. Assembles a management team that could include a COO, department heads, directors of marketing, HR and IT.

3. The firm's visionary; always thinking about the firm's direction and what needs to be done; the firm's champion for strategic planning.

4. Ensures that the firm focuses on growth. The MP doesn't need to be the firm's rainmaker, but he/she plays a major role in coordinating the firm's overall marketing PD efforts.

5. Plays a major, continuing role in making the firm a great place to work; dealing with human relations at all levels.

6. Deals with partner issues of all kinds, including partner relations, teamwork, conflict resolution, coaching and partner mentoring.

7. Holds partners accountable for their performance and behavior.

8. Promotes the firm's culture and gets all personnel, especially the partners, to live and breathe the firm's core values.

9. P&L responsibility for the firm.

10. Leads the firm's efforts to fairly & properly allocate partner income.

11. Gets decisions made promptly.

12. Manages the firm's succession plan.

13. An active leader in the profession and in the community.

Best practices for the MP to focus on

The MP job description on the previous page is a good, traditional way to describe this position. Here are 25 best practices that enable CPA firms to become great firms. No firm rates an "A" on all of them, but outstanding firms do most of them and it's the MP that makes them happen.

1. Proactive business-getting efforts; lots of team selling.	
2. Exploit potential with existing clients.	
3. The power of niche marketing and developing specialized expertise.	
4. World class service.	
5. Be a higher-priced-lower-volume firm rather than vice versa.	
6. Effective management, governance structure & leadership.	
7. Franchised procedures.	
8. Institutionalized clients; selling and servicing done as a team.	
9. Partners mess with clients and staff, staying out of administration.	
10. Survey clients and staff to find out what they think of you.	
11. Maximize staff-partner leverage; partners are delegators, not doers.	
12. Clear strategic plan. Vision. Direction. Implementation.	
13. Right people ON the bus and wrong people OFF the bus; common focus & culture.	
14. Diversity of services.	
15. Tenacious commitment to making your firm a great place to work.	
16. Partners are good bosses that cause staff to stay and get promoted.	
17. Proactive leadership development.	
18. World class training.	
19. Succession planning, including client account transition.	
20. Good partner relations; conflicts addressed.	
21. Partner accountability and good corporate citizenship.	
22. All partners and staff should have goals and targets.	
23. Performance-based partner compensation.	
24. Put technology to work for you.	
25. Benchmarking to improve firm performance.	

Decisions that MPs should make without a partner vote

Tony Kendall is the CEO of Mitchell & Titus, a firm of over 170 professionals, 19 partners and locations in New York City, Chicago, Philadelphia, Newark, Baltimore, and Washington, D.C. Shortly after taking over the reins from the firm's founder, he orchestrated changes in the firm's management structure, saying this:

> "I can't manage this firm if I have to take a vote every time I want to make a decision."

All partners usually vote on the following major decisions:
- Admitting or dismissing a partner.
- Mergers and lateral partner hires.
- Changes to the partnership agreement.
- Expenditures in excess of a dollar amount.
- Annual budget approval.

Beyond the above, most well managed firms with a strong MP allow him/her to make the following decisions without any approval process:

1. Finalizing goals for partners; performance evaluations of partners.
2. Assist with major clients and participate in major prospect pitches.
3. Determine the services to be provided by the firm – leadership role.
4. Staff hiring and termination – leadership role.
5. Staff compensation and benefits – setting overall guidelines.
6. Staff charge hour target guidelines – leadership role.
7. Appoint department and industry specialty heads.
8. Partner retreat planning.
9. Make preliminary, confidential contact with merger candidates.
10. Major technology decisions.
11. Transferring clients between partners.
12. Approval of WIP write-offs above a certain minimum.
13. Client acceptance & retention, including credit holds.
14. Major vendor contract decisions.
15. Spending decisions, in general, to a dollar limit.
16. Insurance policy decisions.
17. Borrowing money – to a dollar limit.

How should the MP spend his/her time?

This is another question that has no magic answer. Activities that vie for the MP's time are:

1. Managing the firm.
2. Rainmaking.
3. Client management.

Recent statistics from The Rosenberg Practice Management Survey show:

Firm Size	Annual Billable Hours		% MP to All
	Managing Partner	All Equity Partners	
Over $20M	632	1,079	59%
$10-20M	736	1,090	67%
$2-10M	959	1,117	85%

Armed with the above, my experience with firms would indicate that the MP's time is spent as follows:

	Over $20M	$10-20M	$2-10M
Managing the firm	54%	38%	21%
Rainmaking	21%	16%	12%
Client management	25%	46%	67%
TOTAL	100%	100%	100%

Managing a large client base and doing billable work that can be delegated to other partners are activities that the best managing partners avoid or minimize. They see the following as their main focus:

- Manage the firm.
- Bring in business.
- Assisting at a very high level in overseeing the firm's largest clients and participating in sales pitches for new, large clients.
- Very small number of billable hours, limited to sophisticated consulting projects with large clients.

How should the MP be compensated?

Ideally, a firm with a "true" MP uses the compensation committee system for allocating partner income. One of the strengths of this system is that it gives the firm flexibility in recognizing the performance of all partners, the roles they play, how well the roles were performed and achievement of goals. Different partners have different strengths in one or more of the following areas:

- Bringing in business.
- Client relationship and engagement duties.
- Truly managing the firm, including service as department heads and committee members.
- Administration (different from management).
- Leading a firm niche or specialty.
- Training staff.
- Mentoring staff.
- Technical expertise in audit or tax.

There is no magic approach or formula that dictates how each of the above should be weighted vs. the others. It's up to the compensation committee to decide this. However, the vast majority of firms compensate the first three items above more than the others.

I've heard that some MPs are compensated partially or totally based on the profits of the firm, but I have not personally seen this once in over 20 years of consulting.

Special factors to be taken into account in compensating the managing partner

1. Other than managing the firm, two performance attributes tend to result in the highest level of compensation: bringing in business and the size of one's billing responsibility (sometimes referred to as book of business). When a partner serves as the MP, he/she reduces the time spent in pursuit of these two activities and, therefore, will post lower production statistics than other partners with little or no management duties.

2. Related to #1 above, the MP may have transferred clients to others to free up the time necessary to perform the MP job.

3. Accomplishments of the MP that led directly to improved profits, such as:

   - Orchestrating a successful merger.
   - Hiring a partner from another firm.
   - Installing a new time and billing system that results in fewer write-offs.
   - Challenging partners on their WIP write-offs, thereby increasing realization.

Who should earn more: the managing partner or the rainmaker?

That depends.

In allocating partner income, a firm needs to look at all performance attributes of each partner. From a 35,000 foot altitude, firms should be reviewing these items for each partner:

1. The partner's role in the firm, the relative *values* of the various roles (MP, rainmaker, client handler, QC expert, niche specialist, administrator, etc.) and how *well* the role was performed.

2. The extent that the partner achieved his/her goals.

There are 3 different roles a partner can play:

- Most partners are client handlers. Excellence in leadership, bringing in business, retaining and profitably growing a client base, helping staff grow, teamwork, interpersonal skills are expected.

- The MP's role focuses on profitability, execution of the strategic plan, holding partners accountable, effective firm governance, overseeing revenue growth, making the firm a great place to work, crisp decision-making and effective succession planning.

- The rainmaker is often the highest paid partner because partners perceive that bringing in business trumps all other performance attributes. But I've seen many rainmakers perform poorly in other important areas such as growing the staff, billing and collection, teamwork and accountability. These need to be taken into account.

It's not enough to ask which of these three roles should be the highest paid. Firms need to look at (a) how well these roles were performed and (b) the "whole package" of performance factors, not just one or two.

How Should The NEW Managing Partner Be Compensated?

Baby boomer partners are rapidly approaching retirement age, resulting in a dramatic increase in new MPs at firms. Many firms are skipping a generation and turning the reins over to "younger" partners. Firms are also asking their new MPs to divest themselves of a significant part of their client base to free up their time to properly manage the firm. How should the new MP be compensated?

Consider the case of a new MP who is relatively young, and his/her comp is 30% below the highest earner. It would be highly unlikely that the newly promoted MP could justify being the highest paid partner in his/her first few years as partner. But few would argue that if this new MP significantly improves the firm's growth and profitability, he/she would be entitled to above-average compensation increases, thereby closing the gap on that 30% pay differential.

Like any job, the scope of the position must first be clarified before compensation can be set. For example:

- Will the new MP be a CEO or merely the administrative partner?
- What will the partners expect of the new MP?

The new MP is taking on a major risk: Will his/her management style be compatible with the other partners? If the new MP sheds clients to carve out time for the MP job, this could jeopardize his/her compensation, both while MP and afterward. To offset this risk, firms typically provide compensation guarantees to protect the new MP.

MANAGING PARTNER EVALUATION FORM

The process

This is really an upward evaluation. Like all upward evaluations, people evaluating the MP should be limited to those in a position to offer informed input. This means that at firms of fewer than 10-15 partners, all the partners will probably want to participate. But once a firm gets beyond 10-15 partners, an increasing number of partners may not be in a position to respond to the evaluation factors listed in the form.

Firms with management or executive committees may wish to limit the evaluation to the partners on those committees.

Once you have decided who will be allowed to participate in the evaluation, each partner should complete an evaluation form. Then, someone should tabulate the forms and summarize the results.

The evaluations should be done on a semi-anonymous basis. Partners' names should be on the forms so that the coordinator of the review process can go back to people for clarification and amplification of responses. But the MP should not have access to who said what.

Related to the above, there needs to be some sort of filtering of negative comments coming from poor performing partners. Partners who consistently fail to perform in certain areas (staff relations, collecting receivables, turning in timesheets, etc.) will more than likely feel that they are in the MPs "doghouse" and may be unfairly hostile to the MP in his/her evaluation. (The same is true, by the way, of staff evaluating their supervisors).

The process should be concluded with a meeting between the MP and a small group of people (no more than three) charged with delivering the results and engaging the MP in a discussion about what his/her goals should be for the next twelve months.

MANAGING PARTNER EVALUATION FORM

Overall rating scale

EE   Always meets expectations and in some areas, exceeds them.

ME   Always meets expectations; this grade is excellent and the MP and the partners alike should be very satisfied with this rating; it should not be viewed as an "average" grade.

NI   Needs improvement in this area

EVALUATION CRITERIA	EE	ME	NI
1. Has the MP assembled and empowered a **management team** that performs at a high level?			
2. How well has the MP functioned as the firm's **visionary**? Has the MP achieved a healthy blend of long-term thinking vs. short-term results?			
3. Does the firm have a written strategic plan? Has the MP been effective at **implementation** of **strategic planning** goals and action steps?			
4. Does the MP keep the bar high on issues of work **quality**, service standards, integrity and ethics?			
5. Is the firm active in **marketing** and selling and does it have a well-articulated plan for **growth**? Has the firm met its goals for growth?			
6. Does the firm truly operate as a **team?**			
7. How effective has the MP been at identifying **merger** candidates and merging them in?			
8. Has the MP addressed and resolved **partner conflicts** swiftly and competently?			
9. Has the MP made an impact on making the firm a **great place to work** where staff retention is high, training effective and recruiting successful?			
10. Has the MP made a meaningful impact on firm **profitability**?			

EVALUATION CRITERIA	EE	ME	NI
11. Are **basic, routine matters** handled efficiently and timely (WIP billed, write-offs challenged, receivables collected, internal financials issues)?			
12. Has the MP held partners **accountable**? Are the partners in the firm truly held accountable for their conduct and performance?			
13. Has the MP's involvement in the **partner compensation and retirement systems** been effective? Do a strong majority of partners feel these systems are reasonable and fair?			
14. Has the MP developed an effective style and approach to **coaching other partners** and helping them develop and succeed?			
15. Does the MP make **decisions** promptly and effectively? Is the MP a good problem solver?			
16. How effective has the MP been at **building consensus** among the partners, where needed?			
17. Does the MP periodically **communicate to the other partners** about what he/she is doing and what's going on in the firm?			
18. Is the MP **visible in the community** and is the firm represented well? Does the MP help the firm maintain a strong public image?			
19. Does the MP **set a good example** to firm personnel for personal conduct? Has the MP been a good role model for the staff?			
20. Has the MP addressed **succession-planning** issues? Is there a plan in place?			
21. Does the MP keep the **shareholders' agreement** current?			

Additional questions

1. What should the MP *start* doing?

_____

_____

2. What should the MP *stop* doing?

_____

_____

3. What should the MP do *more* of?

_____

_____

4. What are 3 things the MP should do next year to improve the firm?
a._____
b.._____
c._____

5. Does the MP do a good job at achieving a proper balance between managing the firm and serving his/her client base?
[ ] Too much time on client base and not enough on management.
[ ] Too much time on management and not enough on client base.
[ ] Balance is good

6. Other comments and suggestions:

_____

_____

_____

5

Key Management Positions

The COO/Firm Administrator

In baseball, the Most Valuable Player award is conferred to superstars of the game. There is controversy over who should win the award: the player with prodigious *individual* production stats or the one player in all of baseball who was the most valuable player *to his team,* who was indispensable, without whom the team would not be a winner.

In a CPA firm, the nominees for the MVP award are:

- The managing partner.
- The rainmaker.
- A great client handler.
- The firm administrator.

Both our experiences with CPA firms as well as the results of several surveys we've done of firm administrators show that FAs can build a very strong case for winning the MVP award.

A survey of firm administrators

In recent years, we have conducted several surveys of firm administrators across the country. The next page summarizes key FA roles that build the case for the FA being his/her firm's MVP:

1. With 90% of managing partners spending only 500-750 hours a year on firm management, that means the FA is usually the *only* member of the firm devoting 100% of his/her energies to managing the firm's #1 client – the firm.

2. The main way that FAs make money for the firm is by keeping partners away from administrative matters, thereby (a) freeing them up to perform like partners (bringing in business, handling client relationships, performing billable work and nurturing the staff, etc.) and (b) performing administrative tasks more skillfully than the partners ever could.

3. FAs possess an impressive portfolio of skills including versatility, leadership, organizational skills, being a good listener, following through on projects, timeliness, having the courage to try new things, people skills and persistence. This is the stuff that MVPs are made of.

4. Most FAs spend fewer than three hours per week with the MP. Performing a long list of diverse duties while spending only three hours a week with the MP evidences the self-sufficiency and dependability of firm administrators.

5. Two-thirds of FAs supervise the preparation of their firm's financial statements. This is incredible when you think about it: a firm full of CPAs entrusting the preparation of their own financials to someone outside their charmed circle. FAs serve not only as their firm's COO but as their CFO as well.

6. FAs contribute significantly to firm profitability by managing expenses. This is an amazing feat because CPA firms are not lavish spenders. Perhaps only 10% of a firm's expenses offer an opportunity for improving profits. But FAs find a way.

7. 80% of FAs are involved in their firm's collections. Partners are notoriously weak at this. But FAs know that huge billings mean nothing unless the bills are collected. And this is where FAs really save the day.

COO / FIRM ADMINISTRATOR
JOB DESCRIPTION

This position is responsible for the following duties, which may be managed, supervised, coordinated or performed directly, depending on the size of the firm and what the firm needs from the position. Most administrators are responsible for most of these duties, but few are responsible for all of them.

1. Internal accounting, financial & operational reporting. Includes budgeting & cash management.

2. Monitor overall profitability. Analyzes financial and operating reports, identifies areas holding profits back, monitors productivity of firm personnel, monitors realization and challenging write-offs, collections and cost control.

3. Staff and HR. Point person for firm recruiting, performance evaluation, salary administration, training, CPE documentation, new employee orientation and benefit administration.

4. Partner activities. Works closely with the MP and the Board. Attends all partner meetings and retreats, plans agendas for partner meetings and monitors implementation of strategic plan goals and action steps.

5. Manages most of the firm's systems. Example: time and billing.

6. Manages or oversees the firm's technology.

7. Manages administrative issues - space planning, high-level landlord issues, policies and procedures and supervision of the admin staff.

8. Property/casualty, benefit and malpractice insurance.

9. Marketing support. Only if there is no marketing director.

10. Mergers. Manages administrative and physical aspects of merging in smaller firms.

HOW THE MP AND COO/FA SHARE
FIRM MANAGEMENT

ACTIVITY	MP	COO/FA
1. Accountability – getting this from partners.	X	
2. Hiring of professionals such as COO/FA, marketing director, etc.	X	
3. Allocation of partner income.	X	
4. Banking– manages the banking relationships.		X
5. Billing rates for all personnel; ensure that rates are revised periodically.	X	
6. Budgeting for the firm.		X
7. Collections; member of admin group makes "soft collection calls."		X
8. Community – represent the firm.	X	
9. Decision-making done promptly.	X	X
10. Department head appointments.	X	
11. Diversify services.	X	
12. Exit interviews – should be conducted for all personnel leaving the firm.		X
13. Goal setting for partners (staff –optional); formal, written, SMART goals.	X	X
14. High level counsel & advice to the MP.		X
15. Hires and supervises admin staff.		X
16. Insurance policies-benefit, liability and property.		X
17. Internal actg; purchasing; pay bills, payroll.		X
18. IT functions.		X
19. Large clients – getting involved at a high level, when necessary.	X	
20. Leadership development and succession planning.	X	
21. MAP conference – attend one or two MAP conferences a year.	X	X

ACTIVITY	MP	COO/FA
22. Major client sales presentations – on "big" sales opportunities.	X	
23. Marketing plan – creation and implementation. Also admin aspects.	X	X
24. Mentoring program-train mentors create plan; assign mentors.		X
25. Mergers.	X	X
26. Negotiation of high level, large transactions such as office space.		X
27. New partners – make nominations to full partner group.	X	
28. Niche marketing & specialties – lead the effort to find champions.	X	
29. Orientation of new employees.		X
30. Partner conflicts – resolving.	X	
31. Partner meetings – plan and lead.	X	X
32. Partnership agreement including retirement plan.	X	
33. Performance appraisal system for the partners	X	
34. Performance appraisal system for the professional staff and admin staff.		X
35. Policies and procedures.		X
36. Practice development – lead the firm's charge; get lots of activity.	X	
37. Production targets – set them.		X
38. Profitability of the firm – high level review and discussion.	X	X
39. Retreat planning; select administrator; set agenda.	X	X
40. Salaries and benefits of all staff		X
41. Scheduling of staff		X
42. Strategic planning.	X	X
43. Transition of retiring partners – coordinate transition of clients.	X	

FIRM ADMINISTRATOR EVOLUTION MATRIX

	Level At Which the COO/FA Operates:		
	Lower Level	**Between Low / High Level**	**Highest Level**
How they function in the firm	Ranges from assistant to the MP to office mgr.	Ranges from office manager to FA.	COO; partner rank; seen by others as a "partner."
Attendance at ptr mtgs and retreats	Never.	May attend but is excused during sensitive discussions	Attends all partner meetings of all types.
Involvement in partner meetings	None.	May attend but usually is very quiet.	As vocal and active as the partners. "When the F/A speaks, partners listen."
Planning of partner meetings	Never.	Some help to the MP	Main planner of the meeting.
Strategic planning & partner goal setting	Never.	Very little.	A vital contributor.
Budgeting	Never.	Very little.	The "keeper."
Analysis of profits & productivity	Never.	Some.	Heavy.
Accounting duties (if qualified)	Hands on book-keeping.	Some hands-on; may supervise accounting staff.	CFO.
Human resources	Never.	Personnel record-keeper, benefits, policy manual, orientation.	Heavy HR: Pro staff recruiting, mentoring programs, staff appraisals.

	Level At Which the COO/FA Operates:		
	Lower Level	**Between Low / High Level**	**Highest Level**
Recruiting & supervision of admin staff	Interviews admin staff; hiring done by partners.	Interviews & hires admin staff; does performance appraisals.	May supervise professional HR, training and IT people in addition to all admin staff
Interviewing professional staff	Never.	Some.	Often.
I.T.	Very little.	Some, depending on the person's I.T. skills.	Little hands on, but ensures that the firm is using technology efficiently
Hands-on duties for coffee and meals at partner mtgs.	Very common.	Some.	No more than any other partner – virtually none.
File room, phones, general office.	Heavy hands on; often backup.	Still important but more supervising of others instead of hands-on.	Supervises but rarely gets fingers dirty
Mergers.	Never.	Some, mostly after the merger is done.	Major role in merger evaluation.
Partner involvement in admin.	Still heavy.	Much less but there is still an important role for partners in admin.	Almost no partner involvement necessary.

MARKETING DIRECTOR
JOB DESCRIPTION

Objective:

Develop and target communications that build awareness of the firm. Support, educate, and monitor staff on marketing strategy and tactics.

Planning
1. Develop and monitor a firm marketing plan.
2. Attend strategic partner meetings.

Client Communications
3. Design and manage a reporting system for regular contacts with clients, referral sources and prospects.
4. Plan and coordinate client seminar presentations.
5. Develop firm promotional materials.
6. Maintain the firm's web site and in general, gain name recognition for the firm through use of social media, the Internet and e-mail.
7. Maintain a mailing list for firm promotional materials.
8. Issue periodic press releases to enhance the firm's image.
9. Coordinate efforts to mail firm newsletters and direct mail pieces.
10. Send referral thank-you notes and congratulatory notes to people mentioned in newspapers and journals.

Education, Training, Firm Marketing Support
11. Educate firm personnel about the firm's services.
12. Conduct in-house marketing and sales training seminars.
13. Identify business/trade associations and civic/charitable organizations that firm members can join.
14. Assist in the drafting of client proposals.
15. Develop and fine-tune a marketing incentive program for staff to bring in business and get active in practice development.
16. Identify opportunities for firm members to deliver speeches.
17. Identify opportunities to write articles for publications.
18. Monitor the practice development efforts of partners and staff.
19. Monitor the competition.

HUMAN RESOURCES DIRECTOR
JOB DESCRIPTION

1. Recruit administrative and professional staff.

2. Coordinate college recruitment program.

3. Maintain personnel files for all firm personnel.

4. Ensure that the firm complies with labor laws.

5. Maintain, communicate and interpret personnel policies & procedures.

6. Administer the firm's staff compensation program.

7. Coordinate the firm's performance feedback and appraisal systems.

8. Provide a safe place for staff to go to on sensitive, confidential issues.

9. Coordinate the firm's benefits programs.

10. Coordinate the firm's new employee orientation program.

11. Coordinate the preparation of job descriptions.

12. Coordinate the firm's training/CPE program.

13. Ensure that termination procedures are properly administered.

14. Periodically, administer employee attitude surveys and analyze results.

15. Keep abreast of developments in the human resources field.

6

CPA Firm Committees

When firms are small or newly formed, the firm's management philosophy is characterized by some or all of the following:

1. Democracy. "We all have a vote & we make decisions as a group."

2. Being a partner means that the partners share profits and duties. "If we all pitch in and take responsibility for a certain area of the firm (admin, staff, quality control, marketing, etc.), our firm will be well-managed and we can save the cost of a firm administrator."

3. Partners are pretty much free to do whatever they want. "We don't need partner accountability because as partners, we are accountable to ourselves."

4. "Eat what you kill" mentality. Partners who earn more bring in the most business and work the most billable hours, and vice versa.

But as firms grow, they find that:

- Democracy doesn't work because organizations can't be managed well if a vote has to be taken every time a decision is needed.

- Management by committee waters down and delays decisions. Equally harmful, when partners do work that can be done by much lower paid people, it takes them away from "partner" work – bringing in business, managing clients and mentoring staff.

- Partner accountability becomes necessary because, partners are just like everyone else in the world: they perform better when they are accountable for results and behavior.

- "Eat what you kill" cripples a firm because partners think and act "I" instead of "we."

Management Committee vs. Executive Committee

A management committee is a group of partners, each of whom has a distinct area of the firm to manage. Examples include admin, HR, marketing, quality control, etc. Usually, one of the members of a MC is the managing partner, though he/she usually functions like an admin partner rather than a true CEO. Management committees are found most often in smaller firms. Management committees are rarely intended to reduce the number of general partner meetings convened by the firm.

As the number of partners increases, it's common for firms to form a committee for each functional area, with each committee consisting of multiple partners and professional staff as well.

An executive committee functions similar to the Board of a corporation. The EC's main duties are oversight of the firm and counsel to the managing partner. EC's are most common at firms with 7-8 or more partners and consist of a relatively small number of partners.. When firms initially form ECs, this may not reduce the number of general partner meetings, but as firms grow beyond a dozen or more partners, most find that fewer general partner meetings are needed.

Well managed firms of more than 10 partners have only two committees:

1. Executive committee. A job description for the EC is on the next page.

2. Compensation committee. A group of partners responsible for allocating partner income. A list of best practices for compensation committees appears on the following page.

EXECUTIVE COMMITTEE

General
When the number of partners in a firm gets too large to involve all partners on all issues, firms create an Executive Committee to work with the Managing Partner on the firm's strategic and high-level governance issues, functioning as a Board.

Specific
1. Provide high-level advice and counsel to the managing partner.
2. Provide assistance to the MP as needed.
3. Administer the firm's system for allocating partner income, with the MP as chairperson.
4. Brainstorm with the MP about various strategic issues and the direction of the firm.
5. Make recommendations to the full partner group for partner nominations.
6. Initiate preliminary discussions about and with merger candidates.
7. Research pros and cons of changing the partnership agreement.
8. Review and analyze the firm's profitability and budget comparisons.
9. Discuss sensitive and confidential problems involving all personnel.
10. Plan periodic meetings of the full partner group, including retreats.
11. Evaluate the performance of the MP; provide feedback to him/her.

Decisions usually reserved for vote of the full partner group

- Mergers.

- Partner promotions, lateral hires and terminations.

- Major capital expenditures.

- Major financial obligations such as the office lease.

- Changes to the partnership agreement, especially compensation and retirement.

CPA FIRM COMPENSATION COMMITTEE
BEST PRACTICES

1. The CC has <u>full reign</u> in deciding the methods and techniques used to allocate income. Their mandate is to allocate partner income in a way that achieves a <u>balance between production and intangibles.</u>

2. The system can only work if the people being judged are willing to <u>trust the judges</u>. Period.

3. <u>Link of compensation with the firm's vision</u>. Partners do what the firm *needs* them to do.

4. Each partner has formal, written goals.

5. Partners must be <u>clear</u> on the CC's "rules" before the year begins.

6. The CC reviews performance data carefully. No "gut feels."

7. If there is <u>no communication</u> between the CC and the partners during the year, it's less likely that partner goals will be achieved.

8. <u>Judgments explained</u> are accepted better than those that are not.

9. <u>Make-up</u> of the committee:
   a. Should be small; MP is a permanent member.
   b. <u>Every</u> member of the CC must be credible to the other partners.
   c. No mandatory rotation.

10. CC has two sets of judgments to make:
    a. Finalize bonus/year-end distribution for this year.
    b. Set bases/draws for next year.

11. Decide if all partners see all partners' income, or not.

12. CC decisions should be final. No appeals. No approval needed.

7

Organization Structures

When I started writing this chapter, I intended to include several traditional organization charts, depicting how firms are structured at various sizes. But as I thought about it, I realized this is nearly impossible. CPA firm structures vary considerably from firm to firm because the firm is managed at the whim of the partners:

- All the partners are essentially officers of the firm. They don't want to report to anyone or be accountable for their performance.

- Each partner has unlimited freedom to operate, spawning the often-heard cliché "the firm is run like a group of sole practitioners practicing under one roof, sharing a firm name, staff and overhead."

- The MP has virtually no authority over other partners.

- Department heads are mostly ceremonial and not expected to *manage* anything.

- Administrators usually report to all the partners.

Firms may operate for years without much structure, enjoying happiness and profitability. Then, seemingly overnight, the firm "hits the wall." Growth slows or stops. Staff turn over. Systems become inefficient. Profits stagnate. For many firms, the "wall" is at the $6-8M annual revenue mark, while others don't experience the slowdown until revenues approach $10M.

Roberto Goizueta, CEO of Coca Cola in the '80s and '90s, described this perfectly:

> "Challenging the status quo when you have been successful is difficult. If you think you will be successful running your business in the next 10 years the way you did the last 10 years, you're out of your mind. To succeed, we have to disturb the present."

The cure for this malady is to get organized, embracing the following.

- A strong leader (the MP) with authority and responsibility.
- Stop requiring a vote every time a decision is needed.
- A strategic plan with partner goals.
- A cohesive, integrated marketing strategy.
- A firm administrator to keep partners out of administration.
- A proactive effort to recruit, retain, train and mentor staff.
- Partner accountability.
- Abandonment of the compensation formula.
- Departmentalization.

Each one of the areas above represents a departure from the way most local firms operate. They can't all be done at once.

So, rather than litter this monograph with an infinite number of traditional organization chart diagrams, the following appear throughout the remainder of this chapter:

- **How CPA Firm Governance Structure Changes as the Firm Gets Larger.** A chart showing how the philosophy of managing a firm changes as it grows from "small" to "large."

- **CPA Firm Organization Chart.** A matrix depicting three different firm sizes and the management positions that are commonly found in each.

- **Why Firms Departmentalize.** This section explains the reasons why firms create departments such as A&A and Tax.

CPA FIRM GOVERNANCE STRUCTURE:
HOW IT CHANGES AS FIRMS GET LARGER

STRUCTURAL ASPECT OF THE FIRM	AS FIRMS GET LARGER IN SIZE:	
	THEY TEND TO MOVE AWAY FROM:	MOVING TOWARD:
Style	Partnership-decentralized decision-making, partners "involved."	Corporate-centralized; decision-making; authority vested in a few partners.
Formality	Loosey-goosey; fewer policies and procedures; group of solos practicing as a firm under one roof.	Tight-ship; more policies and procedures; the firm operates as single unit, with partners adhering to the same core values.
Partner accountability	None	Some
Managing partner	MP really more an admin partner with little responsibility for managing partners and profitability.	More of a CEO, with responsibilities for managing partner performance and P&L.
Other key management positions	Maybe an office manager or low level firm administrator.	COO or high level FA; also likely to have directors for marketing, HR and IT.
Partner committees/ involvement in administration	Common for partners to be heavily involved in firm admin.	Partners stay away from internal duties.
Department heads for A&A, tax, niches, etc.	A little, but these positions are mainly ceremonial and technically-oriented.	More formal with department heads serving as "corporate VPs."
Presence of non-equity partners.	Bar is *lower* for making equity partner; fewer NE partners in small firms.	Bar is *higher* for making equity partner; non-equity partners are very common in larger firms.

STRUCTURAL ASPECT OF THE FIRM	AS FIRMS GET LARGER IN SIZE:	
	THEY TEND TO MOVE AWAY FROM:	MOVING TOWARD:
Partner meetings	Scheduled monthly; attendance often not mandatory.	Quarterly; Exec Comm takes on more solid role. Attendance is mandatory.
Partner meeting agenda	Focus on admin issues.	More strategic; few admin issues.
Partner retreats	Haphazard at best; retreats often like partner meetings.	Convened every year; usually an outside leader. Retreats are strategic.
How decisions are made	Lots of votes.	Few votes. MP has lots of decision-making authority.
Executive committee	Less common; may have a management committee.	More common; functions like a corporate board.
How income is allocated	More likely to see formulas, pay equal, ownership percent.	Dominated by compensation committees
System for bringing in a new partner	Rarely anything consistent.	Highly structured and consistent.
Partner retirement	30% of small firms have no plan. Few make it to the 2nd generation.	95% of firms have a plan; most likely to be multiple of compensation system.
Mandatory retirement	Less common.	More common.
Role of strategic planning	Few do it; almost no success at execution.	Common. Many driven by their strategic plan.
Partner goals	Rare.	More formal.
Partner agreement	Likely to be 20 or more years old.	More likely to be current.

CPA FIRM ORGANIZATION CHART

Position	2-5 Partners/ 8-25 FTEs	6-15 Partners/30-90 FTEs	Large Firms – Over $20M
Partners	Partners manage the firm and make decisions together.	As firms move from bottom to top end of this range: • Partners do less mgmt. • MP makes more decisions alone. • Partner meetings move from monthly to quarterly.	• Partners totally out of mgmt. • Partners reporting to dept. heads. • Limited voting. • Partner focus on clients and staff. That's it!
Managing partner	One partner may have MP title but it's more an admin position.	• Starts leading. • Becomes more than a title. • Often manages large client base. Likely to manage all partners alone. • Reports to EC.	• Becomes more of a CEO. • Much less billable work and client handling. • Relies on mgmt team to manage partners. • Reports to E.C.
Mgmt. committee	Common for each partner to head up an admin area.	Disbands as professional administrators are hired.	Same.
Executive committee (Board)	Too small for EC.	• Functions as high level counsel and overview of the firm & MP. • Most positions are elected.	• Functions as high level counsel and overview of the firm. • More and more, the EC is the mgmt team rather than partners elected at-large.

CPA FIRM ORGANIZATION CHART

	2-5 Partners/ 8-25 FTEs	6-10/15 Partners/30-90 FTEs	Large Firms –Over $20M
Depart-mental-ization	Rarely. Partners are usually generalists.	• Starts happening at larger end of range. Tax usually first to departmentalize; audit follows if firm has a lot of audits. • Most partners may still be generalists. • Most staff still may not be aligned with a dept., but tax has more staff than audit.	• Common for most partners to choose A&A or tax; few generalists. • Partners not allowed to sign both audits and tax returns. • Most staff aligned with a department.
Dept. heads	Same as above.	Dept head is misnomer; these positions are technically driven. The firm needs a go-to person for audit and tax.	• Becomes more like a corporate division VP. • P&L responsibility may or may not be present.
Niche/ Industry leaders	Usually N/A at this size.	Only exists if the firm has a true niche or industry specialty. Many firms at this size don't have this.	Niche leaders co-exist with department heads in a matrix-type organization chart.
PICs of branch offices	Usually N/A at this size.	Most firms at this size are still one-office firms.	If branch size is substantial, office PICs are key members of the firm's management team.

CPA FIRM ORGANIZATION CHART

	2-5 Partners/ 8-25 FTEs	6-10/15 Partners/30-90 FTEs	Large Firms – Over $20M
COO/ FA/ Office mgr.	At higher end of this size range, maybe an O.M. reporting to all partners.	• Low end of range-office mgr. • Mid-range-firm administrator • Top of range could have COO or FA with partner "rank."	• COO, or one of the partners may be the COO or admin partner •May have key reports such as marketing, HR and IT directors.
Marketing	Usually N/A at this size.	• Smaller end of range may start with a marketing coordinator. • Position evolves to a marketing director at larger firm size. • Could report to MP, marketing partner or firm administrator.	• Most common for firm to have a Mktg Dir. with coordinator reporting • Many report direct to MP. • May have Bus. Dev. Dir. reporting
Sales/ business developmt	Usually N/A at this size.	Rare.	Fairly common. May report to marketing director or MP.
Human resources	Usually N/A at this size.	• Common for HR to be part of FA's job. • May have an HR coordinator, reporting to FA.	• Most have a high level HR director on board. • May report to COO or MP.
IT	Usually N/A at this size.	Common for IT to be part of FA's job. May use outside IT firms or hire a low-level IT person internally.	• Most have a high level IT director on board. • Most likely reports to COO.

WHY CPA FIRMS DEPARTMENTALIZE

1. Often driven by partner preferences. Moving staff into the department then occurs because of the specializing partner's need for support.
2. Creating departments makes it easier for the firm to be consistent in how work is performed. Result is higher quality of work.
3. At the higher levels of expertise in either audit or tax, it's not feasible for one person to be an "expert" at both.
4. To reduce liability exposure.
5. CPE requirements in a certain area can be so heavy that it is not feasible to get the necessary training in more than one area.
6. Training becomes more effective because people focus in one area.
7. Technology is another driver; it's hard to be proficient with both tax and audit software.
8. Departmentalization lends itself to working like a firm because partners are more interdependent on one another, which fosters teamwork.
9. It helps with scheduling staff
10. It enables firms to increase their billable utilization of staff.
11. By specializing, the firm is able to better position itself in marketing; cross-selling is easier.
12. It enables the firm to offer specific career paths to those that want them.
13. It helps the firm attract staff.

8

Non-Equity Partners

Non-equity partner position: a growing trend

The use of the non-equity partner position is on the rise in the CPA profession, per The Rosenberg Survey:

	Percentage of firms with non-equity partners			
	> $20M	$10–20M	$2–10M	All Firms
2010	78%	61%	39%	46%
2007	47%		33%	37%

In the mid to late 1990s, a severe staff shortage in the CPA profession developed which, except for a brief respite during the 2008-2011 recession, continues to this day, with no end in sight. Many firms had managers on board that were long time, productive members of their firms with good technical skills. A partner once told me, "We would have heartburn if they left." But, they lacked the leadership and/or business-getting skills to fit the classical definition of partner. As the staff shortage worsened, firms worried about retaining these valuable managers, so they were promoted to partner in droves in the late 90s and early 2000s as a retention tactic.

As the profession moved into the mid 2000s, firms realized that a better option for these managers was to make them non-equity instead of equity partners. Firms would then offer an equity partnership to these individuals if and when they started bringing in business or perhaps managed a large enough client base (mostly delegated to them by equity partners) to warrant this promotion.

How the non-equity partner position is commonly used

1. As a way to ease a partner candidate into full equity partner status. A <u>partner-in-training</u> program.

2. To enable a firm to <u>recognize</u> the stature and contributions of someone who meets all the criteria for being a partner <u>except business origination.</u>

3. A staff retention tactic.

4. For <u>lateral partner hires,</u> to provide both the firm and the new lateral hire an opportunity to <u>get to know each other and satisfy each other that an equity position is mutually beneficial.</u>

5. A title for merged-in retirement-minded partners as well as for retired partners working part time.

How a non-equity partner becomes an equity partner

This varies widely by firm. The two most common scenarios are:

1. The non-equity partner brings in business.
2. The firm "needs" another equity partner to properly manage clients due to growth or a partner retiring.

Why the non-equity partner concept works

1. The firm keeps the bar high for promotion to equity partner, reserving the position for those who <u>drive</u> growth and profits.

2. To the outside world and to the firm's staff, non-equity partners are "partners." Their business cards say "partner", not "non-equity partner." They have responsibility for managing clients. They sign client reports and have access to the firm's financial statements (except for income earned by individual equity partners) and they attend partner meetings and retreats.

How the non-equity partner concept can fail

The non-equity partner concept is doomed if the equity partners make it clear to clients and especially to the firm's staff, that these individuals are not "real" partners. If they are treated like staff, denied participation in partner meetings and see the staff as their peers rather than the equity partners, the non-equity partners feel like second class citizens. The promotion to non-equity partner will feel like a gratuitous gesture, blatantly designed to keep them from leaving the firm.

COMPARISON: EQUITY TO NON-EQUITY PARTNER

Characteristic	Non-Equity Partner	Equity Partner
Buy-in	Almost never.	Yes.
Liability	Almost never.	Yes.
Hold him/herself out as a partner	Yes.	Yes.
Attends partner meetings	Usually.	Yes.
A vote	No (but opinion counts).	Yes.
Determination of compensation	Set subjectively by management. They receive a W-2.	Fits within the partner comp system.
Participation in the firm's profits	Indirectly via an incentive bonus plan.	Yes.
Receive partner retirement benefits?	Almost never, but a few firms allow NE partners to accumulate small amounts.	Yes.
Access to partner compensation data.	Rarely.	Yes unless a "closed" system.
Access to confidential data.	Usually.	Yes.
Signing off on client reports	Some do; some don't. AICPA ethics allow it.	Yes.

9

How Decisions Get Made

<u>Alternative approaches used by firms to make decisions</u>

1. **Management by committee**. Democracy rules. Management decisions are made by all the partners as a group.

   Sometimes, I think the worst word ever invented by man, when it comes to managing a professional service firm, is the word "partner." Unfortunately, to many partners, it means:

   - Royalty; a sign that you've made it; like a professor who receives tenure (can never be terminated).

   - The inalienable right NOT to be accountable.

   - The right to participate and vote on every decision made by the firm. The right to know everything that's going on in the firm, down to the smallest detail.

   Management by committee rarely works. Decisions are watered down and rarely made crisply in a timely manner. Hours and hours of the partner group's time is wasted because of how long it takes to get everyone involved in everything.

2. **Decision-making authority of the Managing Partner or Executive Committee (EC) granted by the partnership agreement**.

The gold standard for the effective management of any organization is to establish a leader (President, Executive Director, Managing Partner, etc.) and bestow the position with a sufficient amount of decision-making authority, as contained in the organization's operating charter or agreement, to manage the entity. CPA firms are no exception.

At CPA firms, the MP and the EC are granted specific authorities in the partnership agreement and are elected by the partners to operate within those authorities. This enables the management of the firm to function efficiently and keeps the partners out of most decision-making. There are a half dozen or so critically important decisions that are usually reserved for a vote of the full partner group. See #4 below for more on this.

3. **Consensus decisions made at a partner meeting without a formal vote.**

   Most firms tell me they rarely take votes. Instead, when a decision needs to be made by the partner group instead of by the MP or EC, the group discusses it and a decision is made by consensus. In the vast majority of cases, the consensus is reached without regard to the fact that some partners may have a larger voting percentage than others.

4. **Formal partner vote.** A handful of critical decisions are commonly specified in the partnership agreement as requiring a formal vote. Examples: making someone a partner, mergers, changing the partnership agreement, major capital expenditures and major financial obligations such as an office lease.

   Most firms conduct most votes on a one-person, one-vote basis despite varying ownership percentages for each partner. The reasons for this are:

   a. If voting is done on an ownership basis, it essentially "disenfranchises" minority owners. Their vote doesn't mean much, and it becomes tantamount to not having a vote at all. When they have no vote, they tend to become disenchanted and cease acting like partners.

b. It gives too much power to the majority owners.

A valid concern with one-person, one-vote is that the "power partners" and/or the most productive partners can be easily ousted from their positions (MP, member of Executive Committee, etc.) by a large block of minority partners, and may be at risk to having their compensation unfairly reduced, having major changes made to the partnership agreement or being expelled from the firm.

Here are some workable solutions to this understandable concern:

- Require a "super-majority" vote on the critical issues listed above. The super-majority might be 2/3, 75% or more.

- If one vote-one person votes are taken on a critical issue, any partner can request that voting be done by ownership pct.

- In certain situations, the partnership agreement can have specific wording that requires the vote of a certain partner or group of partners to pass.

One final note on partner votes: When firms have a small number of partners, probably 3 or fewer, it makes sense to require a unanimous vote on all issues. But once a firm grows beyond 3 partners, requiring a unanimous vote essentially results in each partner having veto power over every decision. Potentially, this could hurt the firm because it may prevent them from making a decision that is clearly good for the firm, but for various self-serving reasons, is not acceptable to one partner. Once firms get to 4 or 5 partners, a super-majority vote usually replaces unanimous voting requirements.

5. Items #2, #3 and #4 are used by virtually all firms that have a MP.

VOTING DECISION GRID

Super-Majority* Of All Partners	Majority (51%) Of All Partners	Executive Committee (Alone)	Managing Partner (Alone)
Change partner agreement.	Relocation of the firm.	Approve the strategic plan.	Establish bank accounts.
Change name of the firm.	Elect EC.	Approve annual budgets.	Obtain insurance.
Admit a new partner.	Elect MP.	Recommendations for new partners.	Borrow money within limits.
Expulsion of a partner.	Partner involvement in other businesses and boards.	Recommendations for mergers.	Capital expenditures within limits.
Declaring a partner permanently disabled.	Working past mandatory retirement age.	Function as the compensation committee.	Establish lines of credit.
Capital calls.		Evaluate MP performance.	Hiring & firing of staff.
Mergers in all directions.		Provide advice to the MP.	Determine staff salaries.
Capital expenditures over a limit.			Resolve ethics & professional standards.
Removal of MP.			Assemble mgmt team.
			Create policies & procedures.

*The most common options are 2/3 or 75%.

10

Partnership Agreements

A partnership agreement (for purposes of this chapter, a "partnership" agreement applies to all legal entities, including corporations *and* partnerships) is a legal document that contains clearly defined terms and conditions of the firm including, but not limited to, each partners' responsibilities, their pay and their roles within the business. It also includes rules and regulations that are to be followed by the partners in the business. It is essential for a CPA firm to have a partnership agreement, regardless of how collegial and friendly the partners are with each other.

A partnership agreement can prevent potential future disagreements that could occur pertaining to the objectives and responsibilities of the firm.

A number of years ago, I was engaged by the managing partner of a firm to draft their first-ever partnership agreement. The firm had three partners: the 57 year old founder, who was a dominant, rainmaking managing partner, and two other younger partners who performed at a much lower level than the founder.

After receiving my draft agreement, the founder decided that he and the firm would be better off without an agreement. One reason he gave for this was that he thought the possibility of the other two partners leaving the firm and taking clients was practically zero. Another reason was that he saw his buyout coming from a larger firm he would eventually merge with, instead of from either of his two junior partners.

I advised him against abandoning the agreement and gave him these reasons:

1. Should the founder die or becomes permanently disabled, if there is no agreement in place, the other two partners might each be legally entitled to 1/3 of the value of the firm, both tangible and intangible. The agreement I drafted provided for his two junior partners to receive 20% of the value of the firm, combined.

2. Should either of the two junior partners leave the firm via withdrawal, termination, retirement, death or disability, if their share of the firm's value is disputed and it gets to a court of law, they would have a good argument for being entitled to 1/3 of the value of the firm.

3. Because this firm was very active merging in smaller practices, future merger candidates may not be willing to merge unless there was a partnership agreement in place.

4. Should the firm promote someone to partner, that person may be reluctant to accept a partnership without an agreement in place.

5. The agreement specifies duties, responsibilities and prohibitions of partners. When these issues are contained in a legally enforceable document, signed by all partners, partners are more likely to adhere to these "rules."

6. The way in which the firm is governed is crystal clear to all parties, thereby minimizing arguments. Examples include:
    a. How partners vote.
    b. How partners are compensated.
    c. Authority of the managing partner.
    d. Determining the capital each partner has in the firm.
    e. Method for new partners buying into the firm.
    f. How departed partners get bought out.

Partnership agreements have two major sections:

- Partner retirement/buyout agreement.
- General partnership agreement – everything *other than* the retirement agreement.

I have seen firms with one document that includes both of the above, and I have seen firms with two separate, though integrated, documents. How this issue is addressed is up to your attorney.

The following clauses, which are not intended to be all-inclusive, represent the major sections of each agreement.

Retirement plan/partner buyout

1. What is paid: Capital only? Deferred compensation only? Both?
2. How is capital payment determined?
3. How is the firm's deferred compensation valued?
4. How is an individual's deferred compensation determined?
5. Payout term of capital and deferred compensation.
6. Will interest be paid on retirement payments?
7. Vesting of deferred compensation.
8. When retirement and withdrawal are allowed.
9. Notice of intent to retire or withdraw.
10. Limits on annual payouts to all partners.
11. Funding of retirement payments.
12. Should retired partner benefits be reduced if his/her clients leave?
13. Client transition requirements and penalties for failure to transition.
14. How deferred compensation payments are impacted by the presence of non-traditional and non-annuity-type services.
15. When deferred compensation payments may begin.
16. Health coverage for retired partners.
17. Tax treatment of payments.
18. Clawback – if the firm is acquired, and the "buyer" provides retirement benefits that are more lucrative that the "seller" currently pays to the retired partners, then those retirees are entitled to share in the improved benefits.

General partner agreement

1. Name of the firm.
2. Capital accounts.
3. How a partner's share of capital is determined.
4. Are capital withdrawals allowed? This includes over-withdrawals on distributions.
5. How a new partner buys in, determining ownership percentage, etc.
6. Voting.
7. What ownership percentage means. What it determines.
8. Managing Partner duties, term of office.
9. Executive and/or management committees: how appointed/elected, duties, term.
10. Partner compensation system.
11. Partner duties.
12. Partner prohibitions.
13. Partner expulsion – what are the grounds, what does an expelled partner forfeit?
14. Liabilities of partners to the firm after termination.
15. Non-compete and non-solicitation.
16. Require periodic physical exams of all partners?
17. Require all partners to provide the MP with a copy of their income tax returns?
18. Death and disability.
19. Non-equity partners.
20. Principals (partner rank for a non-CPA).
21. Mandatory retirement.
22. Part-time partners.
23. What happens if the firm is sold or merged out of existence?
24. Issues that many consider "boiler plate" legal language, addressing issues such as confidentiality, mediation/arbitration and indemnification.

11

The Role of a Partner

One of the most common agenda items at partner retreats I have facilitated is the clarification of what it means to be a partner in the firm. I'm sure I've done this a hundred or more times. Based on the results of these retreat topics, I am constantly revising and updating the handouts contained in this chapter. The remainder of this chapter includes the best of those handouts. There is some overlap among the documents, but each has a different perspective.

WHAT IS A PARTNER?

1. A <u>driver</u> of firm growth, profitability and success.

2. Trustworthiness. This isn't about stealing money. Instead, it's about partners exercising good judgment, never circumventing policies and procedures, resisting the temptation to ignore questionable client practices. Being supportive of decisions made by firm management.

3. Leadership. Partners earn credibility with fellow partners and the staff by being a good role model. Inspiring others to follow your lead. Setting an example because the *firm* is evaluated by <u>your</u> conduct.

4. Manage client relationships and engagements effectively; attentive to their needs; establish strong client loyalty to maximize retention. Move clients upscale & grow their fees. Bill & collect promptly.

5. Train and mentor staff. Don't just be a "nice" partner. You should also help staff develop and advance under your tutelage. Treat them with *at least* as much respect as your clients.

6. Bring in business; contribute to marketing in *some* way; develop and cultivate referral sources.

7. Team player; develop a strong team beneath you; ensure that your largest clients have multiple "touch points" within the firm; share work among business units; refer work to other firm members. Commit to the one-firm concept – clients are the *firm's* clients. Put the firm first. Be willing to assist others.

8. Achieve your written goals. Fulfill your role in the firm.

9. Push work down to staff wherever possible; only do "partner-level" work. Recognize that a partner should work ON the business, not IN it. Keep the staff busy; never assume others are doing it.

10. Live and breathe the firm's core values, <u>every day.</u> Respect the firm, its decisions and its partners.

11. Keep your technical skills sharp; never do work that is beyond your capability. Never stop learning.

12. Be a good corporate citizen. Obey the firm's policies and procedures, even if you don't agree with them. Treat people respectfully. Respond in a timely manner to voice mails, emails, etc.

13. Practice good communications at all levels. Let people know what's going on with you.

14. Commit to the highest possible level of professional ethics.

15. Be accountable for your performance.

16. Be healthy personally.

17. Be fiscally responsible, 24/7; you are never "off duty."

WHAT DO PARTNERS OWE THEIR FIRM?

1. Act like an owner every day, always thinking how to help the firm grow; never coast.

2. Deliver on commitments.

3. Do what's in the firm's best interest and not just yourself. Think "we" not "I." Be a team player. Pitch in when others need your help. No Lone Rangers.

4. Fulfill your role in the firm and what is expected of you; achieve or exceed your goals.

5. Live and breathe the firm's core values, every day.

6. Keep conflicts within the partner group, never confiding in staff or people outside the firm.

7. Always show respect for each other. Treat the staff at least as well as you treat clients.

8. Commitment to self-improvement, right up to the day you retire.

9. Contribute to the firm's practice development efforts by adhering to the concept "you can't not try."

10. Trust your partners and avoid second-guessing them.

11. Develop and nurture the staff, be committed to helping them grow.

12. Only do partner-level work; push down work for staff; look for ways to keep the staff busy.

13. Good corporate citizenship;; follow and defend firm policies & procedures.

14. Retain your clients; give them world class service; bill and collect promptly, every month.

15. Obey all provisions of the partner agreement, including paying out retirement benefits to retired partners.

16. Be accountable.

17. Fiscally responsible, 24/7; you are never "off duty."

18. To be healthy personally.

TEAMWORK – PARTNERS

1. Partners agree on a common vision, goals and a set of firm practices, which are followed by *all* partners, even if each partner doesn't agree 100%.

2. Key firm personnel are viewed as team players, particularly in servicing clients. Clients are viewed as clients of the *firm*, not the *individual*.

3. People rarely go on sales calls alone.

4. No Lone Rangers. Partners make sure they establish multiple "touch points" with the client. A "touch point" is another high level person in the firm that has established a relationship with the client that is valued by that client. If the main partner leaves the firm, the client will remain with the firm because of these "touch points."

5. Clients are freely and willingly transferred to other partners and staff because it's best for the client and/or the firm. There is no hoarding.

6. Internal referrals are made to the firm's niches and service groups; ability and willingness to cross-sell.

7. Whenever one partner asks another partner for help and advice, the other partner responds in a proactive, helpful manner.

8. The assisting partner responds without giving consideration to how their personal earnings will be affected or how late they will have to work to make up for it. Instead, they help out because it's the right thing to do.

9. Partners work hard to establish sound relationships with each other:
   - They make a concerted effort to get along with each other.
   - Partners never surface their disagreements to the staff.
   - Partners meet regularly with each other, formally and informally, to maintain and build relationships with each other.
   - Partners communicate to others what's going on in their worlds.

10. Partner roles are clarified, accepted and understood. They work diligently to carry out those roles.

11. Follows and supports management, resisting "nitpicking" of management's decisions.

12. Partners are accountable to each other and to the firm.

13. Specialists get others involved in their niche or specialty, avoiding the situation in which a partner's retirement means the end of the niche or specialty.

14. Partners and senior staff are doing appropriate level work (i.e., delegating).

15. Develops professional relationships with the staff.

12

Partner Accountability

Partner accountability addresses what is expected of each partner, how partners will be managed so that the expectations are met and what the consequences will be for failure to meet these expectations.

How partners at most firms see accountability

I have interviewed hundreds of partners on partner accountability. I frequently ask them if they would like the firm to *have* partner accountability. The most common response I get, somewhat apocryphal, is: "Yes, I'm all for partner accountability (long pause) as long as it doesn't affect *me!*"

Most partners don't dare share their true attitude towards partner accountability. Revealing this attitude would be tantamount to a professional football player telling his teammates that he doesn't believe in teamwork. Many partners believe the following, to some degree:

> "Once we become a partner, we've made it. We don't *need* to be *managed*. We've proven to the firm that we have the talent, drive and professionalism to manage *ourselves*. No one expects more of a partner than him/herself. Partner accountability might sound good, but it's not necessary for partners."

I developed a saying about partners early in my consulting career that stands as tall today as it did 20 years ago:

"As the partners go, so goes the firm."

There are many important people that make it possible for a firm to be successful. But no one drives the firm's success *anywhere near as much* as the partners. They bring in the business. They supervise client relationships and keep them super-pleased. They train and mentor the staff. And they manage the firm.

There are many reasons why the Top 100 firms are the top performing firms in the country. One important factor is that these firms have partner accountability systems that operate exponentially better than at smaller firms. This totally repudiates the "once we become partner, we've made it" attitude above.

The methods used to attain partner accountability are critically important to a firm's overall management and governance structure.

Our favorite definitions of accountability

"If there are no consequences to *failing* to achieve a goal, then it is less likely that the goal will be accomplished." *(Rosenberg)*

"If people are not prepared to be held accountable for what they do, it is unlikely they will achieve much." *(David Maister)*

The 10 main ways that firms achieve partner accountability

1. Compensation.

2. Agree on a firm vision and strategy.

3. Living and breathing the firm's core values.

4. Peer pressure.

5. Managing partner "meeting" with partners as necessary.

6. Partner goal setting.

7. Partner evaluations including upward evaluations of the partners by the staff.

8. Client satisfaction surveys.

9. Clarify the roles & expectations of each partner, with crystal clarity.

10. The "door."

13

Bringing in a New Partner

Succession planning has hit CPA firms hard. As Baby Boomer partners approach retirement age, they naturally are focusing on who can take their place and eventually write their retirement checks.

There are two primary exit strategies for partners:
1. Sell or merge out of existence.
2. Stay independent, retire and get bought out by younger partners who write the partners' retirement checks with smiles on their faces.

The vast majority prefers method #2, but unfortunately, this option is not available to many partners and firms. For various reasons, these firms have not developed new partners to take their place.

Here is a checklist for what firms need to do to bring in a new partner:

1. Evaluate the staff presently employed and determine the extent that they have the potential to become a partner.
2. Implement programs for developing the leadership, interpersonal, business-getting and technical skills needed to become a partner.
3. Create written criteria for what it takes to be promoted to partner and communicate this document to the staff. See the end of this chapter for a sample document.
4. Decide if the firm should create a non-equity partner position.

5. Decide the vote that a new partner will have.
6. Get the new partner to sign a non-solicitation agreement.
7. Create a partner retirement plan that includes a firm valuation.
8. Decide how to compensate the new partner.
9. Decide how the role of the new partner will change, if at all, from when they were a manager.
10. Structure terms for the buy-in of new partners. This should include:
    a. Buy-in amount.
    b. How the buy-in is paid.
    c. Will the buy-in be paid directly to partners or to the firm?

BRINGING IN A NEW PARTNER
THRESHOLDS AND CORE COMPETENCIES

Intangibles
1. TRUST. Integrity, honesty and sound ethical behavior/judgment
2. Credibility with partners and staff
3. Encourages client confidence: Clients are comfortable calling the partner-potential first rather than the originating partner.
4. Strong work ethic
5. Loyalty and commitment
6. Team player
7. Able to pass the "beer/wine" test
8. Communication and interpersonal skills
9. Leadership skills

Financial and legal
1. Is willing and able to buy in
2. Is willing to take on retirement obligation
3. Is willing to sign a non-solicitation agreement
4. Demonstrates personal financial stability

Practice development
1. Originates X amount of business
2. Constantly pursues meetings with clients, prospects and referral sources to get new business
3. Actively seeks opportunities to cross-sell additional services to existing clients
4. Has been active for at least several years in building up network of business contacts
5. Has distinguished him/herself as an expert in at least one service or industry

Production and client management
1. Manages X number of clients (billing, relationship and engagement management)
2. Achieves X billable hours...
3. ...at X realization

<u>Technical</u>
1. Demonstrates a high-level of analytical and problem-solving skills; solves clients' problems
2. Exhibits high level of technical skill so the firm is comfortable that once the partner candidate has finished a client project, no one else needs to review it to make sure it was done right. Candidate has proven his/her ability to complete highly technical projects with minimal assistance from others.

<u>Supervision</u>
1. Has solid experience supervising staff
2. Is a delegator
3. Is able to develop others

<u>Administration</u>
1. Follows and complies with all firm policies, procedures and deadlines

14

Partner Compensation and Retirement Systems

Partner compensation

If you ask the partners, they will tell you that the most critical and sensitive aspect of CPA firm practice management is the allocation of partner income.

Because of the sensitivity of partner compensation, firms change various aspects of their allocation system quite often. For this reason, we strongly advise firms to include wording in their partnership agreements on partner compensation that is very short and quite general. This way, the firm doesn't have to revise the partnership agreement every time a change is made.

Here is a checklist of decisions that the firm needs to make about the method it will use to determine the compensation of each partner:

1. What compensation system will be used?
    a. Managing partner decides each partner's pay.
    b. Compensation committee – a small number of partners determines the compensation of all partners.
    c. Formula – an algebraic formula is devised to compensate each partner for various aspects of performance, primarily business origination, billing responsibility and billable time.

d. Paper and Pencil – each partner allocates partner income as he/she sees fit, the ballots are averaged and the result is how income is allocated.

e. Ownership percentage – income is allocated based on each partner's ownership percentage in the firm.

f. Pay equal – income is split equally among all partners or *mostly* split equally.

g. All partners decide – all partners meet to discuss allocating the income to each partner.

2. Number of compensation tiers, how large each tier should be and who decides this:

   a. The most common tiers are:
      i. Return on capital.
      ii. Base salary or draw.
      iii. Incentive bonus or year-end distribution.

   b. Alternatives for deciding the tiers and the amount of the tiers are commonly decided by:
      i. Compensation committee.
      ii. Vote of all partners.
      iii. Managing partner.
      iv. Executive committee.

3. Performance criteria used to evaluate and compensate each partner.

4. Extent that performance criteria for partners include intangibles.

5. If interest on capital, will it be paid on capital only or capital plus goodwill?

6. Role of ownership percentage, if any.

7. Role of seniority, if any.

8. If there is a base and a bonus:

   a. Will the base be a draw on a final amount for each partner, with the "bonus" being a final distribution to arrive at each partner's income number?

   b. Will the base and bonus be independent of each other so that the bonus is a true incentive bonus?

9. If there is a compensation committee, how many members, how will they be selected, terms, limit of consecutive terms, etc?

10. Appeal procedures of compensation committee decisions, if any.

11. Approval of compensation committee decisions required by the full partner group, if any.

12. Link of compensation to strategic planning.
13. Formal written goals and extent that they will be linked to compensation.
14. Formal, written partner evaluations and extent they will be used to determine compensation.
15. Special impact of the MP on compensation, if any.
16. Mechanisms in place to prevent hoarding of clients and billable hours by partners to maximize their income.
17. Communications to partners regarding criteria used to determine their compensation.
18. For multi-office firms, what has the biggest impact on individual partner income: firmwide profits or local office profits?
19. Interoffice pricing.
20. Closed or open system?

Partner Retirement/Buyout

If partner compensation is THE most critical and sensitive aspect of CPA firm practice management, a close second is partner retirement/buyout – the money partners receive for the purchase of their ownership in the firm when they retire or leave the firm due to death, disability, withdrawal or expulsion.

The amount of money involved is quite significant. Roughly 80% of all firms consider the value of the firm to include:

- Tangible accrual basis capital.
- Goodwill of the firm, usually valued at 75-100% of the firm's annual net fees.

To illustrate, assume that one partner from a five partner firm retires. The firm has annual net fees of $6 million and accrual basis capital is $1.5 million, for a total value of $7.5 million (assume the fees are valued at one times fees). If the retiring partner is a 30% owner, he/she might be entitled to $2.25 million, depending on a variety of variables, paid out over a number of years.

As you can see, the amount of money involved is quite substantial, which explains why partner retirement is such a critically important aspect of firm governance.

The next page is one of the most often-used and requested handouts in my consulting practice. It lists 24 major issues that comprise a properly prepared partner retirement agreement.

PARTNER RETIREMENT/BUYOUT SYSTEMS: WHAT FIRMS ARE DOING

TERMS	WHAT FIRMS ARE DOING
Capital	
1. Total capital defined	Mostly accrual basis capital; some cash basis
2. Payout period	5-10 years
3. Interest on payments?	Almost all firms
4. Individual share determined	(1) Partnership accounting, (2) Ownership percentage or (3) Relative compensation
Goodwill	
1. The math must work.	When a partner retires, the remaining partners' income goes up or remains the same, not down.
2. Pegged to multiple of fees?	80% is average; 100% still common
3. Determination of individual goodwill amounts	• Most use a multiple of comp, say 3 times • Some firms use incremental growth (AAV) • Some use owner % or book of business • Avoid penalizing pre-retirement partner for transitioning clients to other partners.
4. Role of firm ownership	Virtually none
5. Term of payout	10 years is very common
6. Interest on benefits?	Never
7. Vesting	Many variations: • Many make it age-based as well as years as a partner-based. • Most common for full vesting: 10-20 years • Grandfathering sometimes necessary.
8. Age for 100% vesting	Ranges from 60 to 66; trend is to go back up.
9. When retirement allowed	Most allow it at any time. Some firms require a minimum age, say 50 or 55.
10. Notice required	One year very common; moving to two years.
11. Retirement mandatory?	Most firms have this at 65 or 66, with provision that if a partner wishes to continue, annual approval is needed. Partners working past mandatory age usually required to redeem their equity.

TERMS	WHAT FIRMS ARE DOING
12. When payments start if partner withdraws	Most begin payments when a partner withdraws. Some make partner wait until 55 or so.
13. Funding	Very little except for life insurance.
14. Reduce benefits if clients leave?	80% of firms do not reduce; 20% do. The key is to tie receipt of goodwill-based benefits to compliance with client transition practices.
15. Client transition practices	Very weak. Best is: No transition – no goodwill. Institutionalization of clients from the day a company becomes a client, is best practice.
16. Non-traditional and/or non-annuity-type services	Many firms do not pay if services walk away when partner retires. Key: Have the special services been "institutionalized?"
17. Retired partners working part time	Most firms are case-by case. Common practice is to pay 40% of billable time collected.
18. Health coverage	When Medicare kicks in, partner required to join. Early retirement – covered by the firm but partner reimburses the firm for premiums.
19. Tax treatment of goodwill payments	Deductible by firm; regular income to retiree.
20. Death and disability	Most treat these events the same as regular retirement.
21. Disability – continuation of partner's comp	Until disability policy kicks in or until disability is official this is common: 100-75-50-25 common; no pay after one year.
22. Withdrawing partners	Must pay firm 100-125% of fees for clients/staff taken.
23. What causes loss of vested benefits?	Expulsion? Taking clients? Joining another accounting firm?
24. Clawback	If during payout period to a retired partner, the firm is sold for better terms that the firm's retirement plan, retired partners partake in more attractive terms, with a 5 year phase-out.

15

Strategic Planning

Thus far, this monograph has driven home the point that a CPA firm's management and system of governance is comprised of several critical elements. Firms must decide if they want:

- A corporate or partnership form of governance.

- A Managing Partner functioning as a strong CEO **or** one that is more an administrative partner that "keeps the peace."

- An Executive Committee that functions like a Board **or** a Management Committee that performs day to day management and administrative work in lieu of a high level, professional firm administrator.

- An organization structure that specifies where each partner fits in the overall organization and clarifies the role of each partner **or** a structure that grants partners the freedom to adopt their own roles. Will the firm be departmentalized?

- Partner accountability and if so, how will it be attained?

- Partner compensation and retirement systems that are performance-based.

This chapter addresses another important choice that works in unison with the above: What role will strategic plan play in firm management?

Strategic planning definitions

Let's be sure we understand the definition of some key terms:

Strategic planning is the <u>process</u> of examining where you are now, where you want to be, and most importantly, what you need to do to get there. It's a process that never ends. The plan is constantly monitored, changed and revised as circumstances dictate. Strategic planning gets all firm personnel pulling in the same direction. People are energized by knowing their firm has a grand plan, knows where it's going, and is innovative and forward thinking.

See page 9 for a flowchart on a CPA firm's overall management philosophy.

A **vision** is a series of <u>very specific statements that describe what the firm will look like in the future (roughly 5 years)</u>. Examples:

- Develop a specialty in the auto industry.
- Create a firmwide marketing plan that will result in 10% annual growth.
- Merge in two smaller firms in the next five years.

The vision statement drives the creation of the firm's strategic plan document, which is broken down into goals that are assigned to partners and other key personnel.

For a more thorough exploration of strategic planning, read our monograph entitled ***"Strategic Planning And Goal Setting For Results."***

How strategic planning impacts firm management and governance

Firms have two choices for determining the role of strategic planning in firm management and governance:

Choice #1: The vision and strategic plan is the highest level management initiative in the firm – it <u>drives</u> the firm. Management focuses the partners' attention on achieving their role in executing the strategic plan. There is accountability (see Chapter 12) for partners to achieve these goals. Partner production is also very important, but the partners' production efforts must be consistent with the strategic plan.

Choice #2: Nothing is more important than partner production (primarily bringing in clients, building a book of business, billable hours and realization) because this is how firms make good money. The partners are encouraged to work as a team, and there may be a few instances of effective teamwork, but for the most part, partner production is the result of <u>individual</u> efforts to achieve the firm's overall revenue and profit goals (perhaps revenue growth of 10% and income per partner of $400,000).

While partner production is the #1 driver, the firm may still devote a lot of time and energy to the creation of a vision and strategic plan. However, strategic planning clearly takes a back seat to partner production.

16

Profitability

In our monograph, *"What* Really *Makes CPA Firms Profitable,"* we cite several dozen ways to improve profitability. The following tactics have the <u>highest</u> impact on profitability:

1. Drive top-line revenues and stop worrying about expenses. Increased revenues drop directly to the bottom line (profits) whereas costs in a CPA firm are mostly fixed and difficult to trim back.

2. Leverage, as measured by fees per partner and the ratio of professional staff to partner. The goal is for partners to generate multiple hours of work for firm personnel for every hour of their own work.

3. Aggressive billing rates. Clients should think of your firm as "expensive but good." In the CPA industry, firms will be more profitable as a higher rate-lower volume business than a low rate-high volume operation.

4. Productivity in terms of annual billable hours for firm personnel, efficient processes for client work and effective use of technology.

Other tactics for improving firm profitability are:

5. Specialization. Revenue is easier to generate when you are an expert; also, clients are willing to pay more money for expertise.

6. Hire a high level, professional firm administrator to keep the partners out of administration.

7. Challenge WIP write-offs over a threshold amount. A small increase in realization drops directly to the bottom line.

8. Benchmarking, which helps the firm identify areas of the firm that need improvement.

But there is one thing that has a more profound effect on profitability than all eight of the above tactics combined – strong, effective firm management.

The eight tactics listed above don't happen just because some consultant suggests them to you. It takes management to initiate and drive them. Here are some examples:

- To generate revenues, a marketing plan must be created and *implemented*, a diverse portfolio of services are needed to satisfy client needs and partners must be held accountable for practice development. *Management initiates and drives these efforts.*

- To achieve a high staff to partner ratio, partners must delegate staff-level work to staff. To perform this work, talented staff must be recruited, trained well, motivated and retained. The partners execute these actions, *but management initiates and drives these efforts.*

- To develop specialties, they need to be identified and profitably grown. Partners must develop expertise. The specialties need to be marketed. Although individual partners evolve to become specialists, *management initiates and drives these efforts.*

Good management and leadership:

1. Identifies challenges and focuses people's attention on those challenges.

2. Is visionary in its thinking. Leaders constantly find new things the firm needs to do.

3. Persuades people to do what they don't want to do, or do what they're too lazy to do, and like it. (Harry Truman)

4. Holds people accountable for their performance.

5. Makes decisions crisply.

Specifically, in a CPA firm, good management makes sure the firm:

1. Has a strategic plan.

2. Provides services that clients want and need.

3. Markets proactively.

4. Has a means of holding partners accountable for their performance.

5. Tends to the basics–quality control, billing, collection, profitability, productivity, etc.

6. Has good partner relations.

7. Provides an attractive place for staff to work and stay.

A firm's strong management, through the managing partner and other members of the management team, influences the behavior of others to get them to accomplish the above. **There is no greater way to impact the bottom line than strong, management of the firm.**

17

Partner Communications

No organization can flourish over the long term without effective communication among the key people (in our case, the partners). CPA firms are no exception.

Here are some examples of good communication among partners:

1. Formal gatherings, primarily partner meetings and retreats, are scheduled regularly. Both sessions are effectively run. The next page presents a guide for planning effective partner meetings.

2. Informal, ad hoc meetings take place among partners,, further strengthening their relationships.

3. Management, especially the Managing Partner and the Executive Committee, regularly communicates what's going on in the firm.

4. Partners talk to each other in person when important matters are at hand, instead of using impersonal forms such as email and voice mail.

PLANNING EFFECTIVE PARTNER MEETINGS

Format of meetings

1. Set meeting dates a year in advance.

2. An agenda is distributed 10 days in advance of the meeting.

3. Minutes of the meeting are taken and distributed to partners within two days after the meeting.

4. All meetings begin with a review of previous month's "to do" list to determine progress and achieve accountability.

5. All meetings should end with the compilation of a "to do" list, with specific individual(s) assigned to each action item.

6. Attendance at all partner meetings should be mandatory.

7. The COO/firm administrator should attend. If the partners feel this is not appropriate, then you have the wrong person in that role.

Overall focus of the meeting

- Partner meetings should be limited to high-level, strategic issues and discussions. Meetings that are dominated by minor administrative issues will get bogged down, will be boring for most partners and will detract from the strategic focus that needs to be observed.

- Prioritize the agenda items. Address first things first; resist doing the *easiest* things first.

- Partner meetings are a great way to achieve partner accountability through peer pressure. Partners should at all times be respectful and tactful. But, if a partner is neglecting something important and is letting the firm down, partner meetings are an excellent forum for other partners to speak up these instances.

Typical Agenda Items at Partner Meetings

1. Review the "to do" list from the previous meeting – always should be the first agenda item.

2. Review the latest financial results. Focus on what the numbers *mean* and what needs to be *done* rather than a detailed (typical accountants approach) review and challenging of the numbers.

3. Progress on the firm's marketing plan, marketing opportunities and initiatives. Continual focus needs to be on the things that partners are doing to be active and effective at bringing in business.

4. Progress on *implementing* the firm's strategic plan.

5. Status of merger talks and opportunities.

6. *Major* collection and WIP problems.

7. Scheduling of engagements (only if the partners want to use this meeting to do scheduling).

8. Policy and procedures – changes, additions, clarifications (major items only).

9. Major problems in the firm.

10. Planning of future events such as seminars, workshops, retreats and firm social events.

11. High level discussion of the firm's major people issues: Recruiting, performance issues, compensation and benefits, performance evaluations, and promotions.

12. Major financial expenditures.

13. Administrative update (quick; highlights only; avoid endless discussions about minor issues).

18

Conclusion

Of the 45,000 CPA firms in the U.S., an elite group of these firms, referred to as The Top 100 (in terms of annual revenues), is publicized by several media groups. These firms enjoy dramatically higher profitability, as measured by income per equity partner, than the other 44,900 firms. The average income per equity partner of the Top 100 firms, excluding the Big 4, averages roughly $600,000.

Is there one single factor that has enabled these firms to earn membership in this exclusive Top 100 "club?" Some good guesses might be:

- Lots of rainmakers.
- World class service to clients.
- Unparalleled expertise.
- Great talent and the firm's ability to retain and grow that talent.
- High levels of productivity and efficiency.
- Strong, unified culture and devotion to a set of core values.

But I will argue that THE single most important factor to the success of Top 100 firms is strong, effective management and leadership. The reason for this is simple: Strong management makes all the other things happen.